WILLIE MAYS
CENTER FIELDER

SAN FRANCISCO
GIANTS

BARRY BONDS
LEFT FIELDER

SAN FRANCISCO
GIANTS

THE STORY OF THE SAN FRANCISCO GIANTS

Published by Creative Education
P.O. Box 227, Mankato, Minnesota 56002
Creative Education is an imprint of The Creative Company
www.thecreativecompany.us

Design and production by Blue Design
Art direction by Rita Marshall
Printed by Corporate Graphics in the United States of America

Photographs by AP Images, Getty Images (APA, Chicago History Museum, Monica Davey/AFP, Diamond Images, Dennis Desprois/MLB Photos, Mitchell Funk, Jeff Haynes/AFP, Jed Jacobsohn, Paul Kitagaki Jr./ Sacramento Bee/MCT, Mitchell Layton, Brad Mangin/MLB Photos, Peter Read Miller/Sports Illustrated, MLB Photos, National Baseball Hall of Fame Library/MLB Photos, Olen Collection/Diamond Images, Photo File, Rich Pilling/MLB Photos, Mark Rucker/Transcendental Graphics, Don Smith/MLB Photos, Justin Sullivan, Al Tielemans/Sports Illustrated, Tony Tomsic/Wireimage, Ron Vesely/MLB Photos)

Library of Congress Cataloging-in-Publication Data

Goodman, Michael E.
The story of the San Francisco Giants / by Michael E. Goodman.
p. cm. — (Baseball: the great American game)
Includes index.
Summary: The history of the San Francisco Giants professional baseball team from its inaugural 1883 season in New York to today, spotlighting the team's greatest players and most memorable moments.
ISBN 978-1-60818-055-4
1. San Francisco Giants (Baseball team)—History—Juvenile literature. I. Title. II. Series.

GV875.S34G67 2010
796.357'640979461—dc22   2010025220

CPSIA: 110310 PO1381

First Edition
9 8 7 6 5 4 3 2 1

Page 3: Pitcher Amos Rusie
Page 4: Catcher Buster Posey

BASEBALL: THE GREAT AMERICAN GAME

THE STORY OF THE SAN FRANCISCO GIANTS

Michael E. Goodman

CREATIVE EDUCATION

CONTENTS

GIANTS ON THE MOVE

In 1776, a Spanish mission was established by Franciscan monks on the West Coast of the United States in what is now northern California. This settlement was named Yerba Buena, Spanish for "good herb," on account of an herb that grew there and was used as medicine. Eventually, Yerba Buena was renamed San Francisco, after Saint Francis. The town grew slowly for 72 years until gold was discovered nearby in 1848. Then, over the next 18 months, thousands upon thousands of gold-seeking "Forty-niners" poured into the area, quickly turning San Francisco into the largest American city west of the Mississippi River.

Only a few of the new arrivals struck it rich, but most stayed in the area and helped build it up into a great cultural and economic center. More than 100 years later, in 1958, a new migration occurred when the Giants and Dodgers of professional baseball's National League (NL) decided to move west from their original homes in New York City—the Giants settling in San Francisco and the Dodgers in Los Angeles. The

Long known as a fashionable city, San Francisco represented an attractive destination when big-league baseball started to spread west.

PITCHER · CHRISTY MATHEWSON

A powerful right-hander, "Matty" routinely tied batters in knots with his baffling fadeaway pitch. The Giants' all-time leader in earned-run average (ERA), shutouts, wins, complete games, strikeouts, and innings pitched, Mathewson posted 4 seasons with 30 or more wins during his career. Along with greats Honus Wagner, Walter Johnson, Babe Ruth, and Ty Cobb, Mathewson was part of the initial induction class into the Baseball Hall of Fame. A college-educated man, Mathewson was also an accomplished checkers player, and he once beat world champion Newell Banks, who reigned as checkers king from 1917 to 1922 and from 1933 to 1934.

CHRISTY MATHEWSON
PITCHER

SAN FRANCISCO
GIANTS

STATS

Giants seasons: 1900–16

Height: 6-foot-1

Weight: 195

- 2,507 career strikeouts

- 12 consecutive 20-win seasons

- 2.13 career ERA

- Baseball Hall of Fame inductee (1936)

relocations meant that, for the first time, major league baseball would be played from coast to coast.

The Giants brought a long history and a winning tradition with them to San Francisco. The club had been formed in 1883 as the Gothams, and it played its first games just north of New York's Central Park on a field that had once been used for polo games. From then on, that field and a stadium later built a little farther north were known as the Polo Grounds.

In 1885, the Gothams made a strong run at the NL pennant, finishing 2 games behind the powerful Chicago Cubs after winning 85 games and losing only 27, a remarkable .759 winning percentage. Pitchers Tim Keefe and Mickey Welch combined for 76 of the team's wins, and first baseman Roger Connor batted a league-leading .371. According to legend, New York manager Jim Mutrie was so thrilled by his team's success that he greeted them in the dugout one day as "My big fellows, my giants." The new name caught on with sportswriters and fans.

The Giants won their first pennant in 1888, led by Connor, Keefe, and future Hall-of-Famer Buck Ewing, who is considered by many baseball historians to be the best catcher of the 19th century. Ewing

JOHN McGRAW

John McGraw had a "win-at-any-cost" mentality and was known to use dirty tactics in his defense and base running.

had a quick bat, a rocket arm, and surprising speed. He was also fiercely competitive. "He used to sit up at night thinking about ways to upset and beat his rivals of the next day," Welch recalled. "He originated the pre-game clubhouse meeting. He'd do anything to win."

Ewing's Giants won a second straight pennant in 1889, then fell in the standings during the 1890s, despite the heroics of pitcher Amos Rusie and shortstop George Davis. Rusie won 20 or more games 8 times during the decade, including 4 straight 30-win seasons. Davis batted .300 or better nine times and was almost as outstanding in the field. But both stars were constantly at odds with Giants owner Andrew Freedman, who was known as both a tightwad and a tyrant. Most sports fans in New York disliked Freedman, and they were thrilled when he sold the team to businessman John Brush in 1902.

The club that Brush bought featured a secret weapon—feisty, hardnosed infielder John McGraw, who signed with the Giants as a player/manager just before Brush made his purchase. McGraw would hold the reins of the team for the next 31 years and help change the face of baseball in the first part of the new century.

POLO GROUNDS

The famous Polo Grounds served as the home field at various times for no fewer than four different big-league franchises. This photo shows the park in 1895, when everyday transportation meant horse and buggy.

A RIVALRY IS BORN

After the Giants won their second straight NL pennant in 1889, they faced off against the champions of the American Association, the Brooklyn Bridegrooms, in the 19th-century version of the World Series. The Giants won the series 6 games to 3, and a rivalry was born that has lasted more than 120 years. The Bridegrooms, who were later renamed the Dodgers, joined the Giants in the NL in 1890, and the two clubs engaged in many exciting pennant races over the years, first in New York City and later on the West Coast, where they moved together in 1958. The players and fans of both clubs have always felt the intensity of the rivalry. In April 1925, Brooklyn team president Charles Ebbets died on the morning a Giants–Dodgers series was scheduled to begin. The games went on as scheduled because, as Brooklyn manager Wilbert Robinson said, "Charley wouldn't want anybody to miss a Giant–Brooklyn series just because he died." One man who truly understood the rivalry was fiery manager Leo Durocher. Durocher's Dodgers teams consistently pounded the Giants in the late 1940s. Then, as Giants manager in 1951, he oversaw New York's amazing comeback to overtake Brooklyn for the NL pennant that year.

CATCHER · BUCK EWING

A terror behind the plate, William "Buck" Ewing's cannon arm could throw out would-be base stealers even while he remained in his catcher's crouch. With a bat in his hand, he was just as fearsome. In his rookie year, Ewing hit three triples in one game and became the first major-league player ever to hit 10 home runs in a season. He hit .300 or better 11 times as a professional, and in 1900 he co-managed the Giants with shortstop George Davis. Ewing was considered a "complete" ballplayer, also logging time in the outfield, at all of the infield positions, and on the pitcher's mound.

BUCK EWING
CATCHER

SAN FRANCISCO
GIANTS

STATS

Giants seasons: 1883–92

Height: 5-foot-10

Weight: 188

- **1,625 career hits**

- **.303 career BA**

- **354 career stolen bases**

- **Baseball Hall of Fame inductee (1939)**

GIANTS

FIRST BASEMAN · WILLIE McCOVEY

Willie "Stretch" McCovey exploded onto the big-league scene in 1959, as his .354 batting average and winsome personality earned him the NL Rookie of the Year award. McCovey's sweeping swing was the envy of the majors, and he racked up more than 500 dingers and 2,200 hits throughout his career. He was given a permanent place of honor at the Giants' modern home stadium when McCovey Cove, the waters behind the right-field wall of AT&T Park, was named after him. McCovey's number 44 uniform, which he wore in honor of fellow Alabamian and former home run king Hank Aaron, was retired by the Giants in 1981.

WILLIE McCOVEY
FIRST BASEMAN

SAN FRANCISCO
GIANTS

STATS

Giants seasons: 1959–73, 1977–80

Height: 6-foot-4

Weight: 210

- 6-time All-Star

- 18 career grand slams

- 521 career HR

- Baseball Hall of Fame inductee (1986)

MASTERFUL McGRAW

 cGraw's gruff, dictatorial manner earned him the nickname "Little Napoleon," and, like the notorious French emperor, he had great ambition and self-confidence. "The main idea is to win," he said, "and we will win as long as my brains hold out."

McGraw used a combination of brains and bullying to drive his team. Within two years, he pushed the Giants all the way to the 1904 NL pennant with a 106–47 record. McGraw knew he had phenomenal talent at his disposal, especially on the mound. Joe "Iron Man" McGinnity threw 38 complete games in 1904 and won 35 of them. Crafty right-hander Christy Mathewson was not far behind with 33 victories and also led the league in strikeouts. Mathewson's secret weapon was a pitch he called the "fadeaway," a slow-moving curveball that broke right instead of left.

The Giants were NL champions but refused to take on the Boston Pilgrims of the American League (AL) in a World Series that year. McGraw had a grudge against Ban Johnson, the AL president, and announced that because of Johnson's "crookedness," the Giants would not play any more games that year.

McGraw relented the next season and agreed to play in the World Series after his team won another NL pennant behind Mathewson's 31 wins. Using a combination of dominant pitching and clutch hitting, New York defeated the AL champion Philadelphia Athletics four games to one, and all four victories were shutouts, three by Mathewson. "Mathewson was the greatest pitcher who ever lived," said legendary Athletics manager Connie Mack a few years later. "It was wonderful to watch him pitch—when he wasn't pitching against you."

Over the next 20 years, McGraw continued to push his players, and the team continued to win. The Giants captured three straight NL pennants in 1911, 1912, and 1913 and another in 1917 but came up short in the World Series all four times. The team's success continued into the early 1920s, sparked by clutch-hitting outfielder Irish Meusel and speedy second baseman Frankie Frisch. The Giants won an additional four straight pennants from 1921 to 1924 and topped the New York Yankees in the World Series in both 1921 and 1922.

JOE McGINNITY

SECOND BASEMAN · # JEFF KENT

Jeff Kent never settled for less than his best—perhaps that was why he made it to the postseason seven times over the course of his career. The intense second-sacker had a banner season in 2000, when he assembled a career-high .334 batting average and won the NL Most Valuable Player (MVP) award. Although Kent was known to squabble with his teammates on occasion, he could always be relied on to perform at the plate. While in San Francisco, Kent posted more than 100 RBI each season and even batted for the rare cycle on May 3, 1999, hitting a single, double, triple, and home run against the Pittsburgh Pirates.

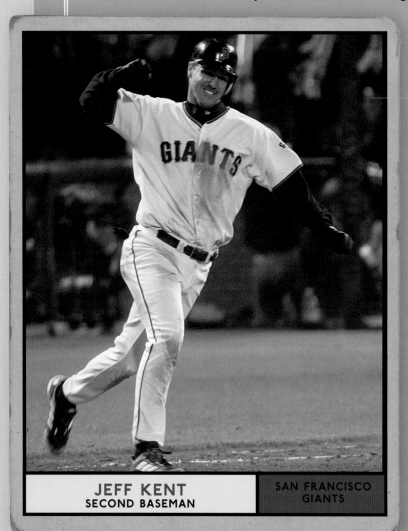

JEFF KENT
SECOND BASEMAN

SAN FRANCISCO
GIANTS

STATS

Giants seasons: 1997–2002

Height: 6-foot-1

Weight: 205

- **5-time All-Star**

- **2,461 career hits**

- **1,518 career RBI**

- **560 career doubles**

After capturing the 1924 NL pennant but falling in the World Series to the Washington Senators, the Giants lost their winning touch. When the club dropped to sixth place early in the 1932 season, McGraw—feeling physically and emotionally drained—decided to retire. Less than 2 years later, he died at age 60. At McGraw's Hall of Fame induction in 1937, Connie Mack said, "There has been only one manager, and his name is John McGraw."

When first baseman Bill Terry replaced McGraw as player/manager in 1932, he had several stars in his lineup, including himself. Terry was a lifetime .341 hitter and an outstanding fielder. He was backed on offense by right fielder Mel Ott, who could generate amazing power with his odd "foot-in-the-bucket" step, so named because, as the pitch approached, he lifted his right foot as if he were stepping into a bucket. Leading a solid pitching staff was "King Carl" Hubbell, a crafty lefty with terrific control, and "Prince Hal" Schumacher, a flamethrowing right-hander.

Before the 1933 season began, Terry predicted that the club would finish "third or better." The Giants surpassed Terry's expectations,

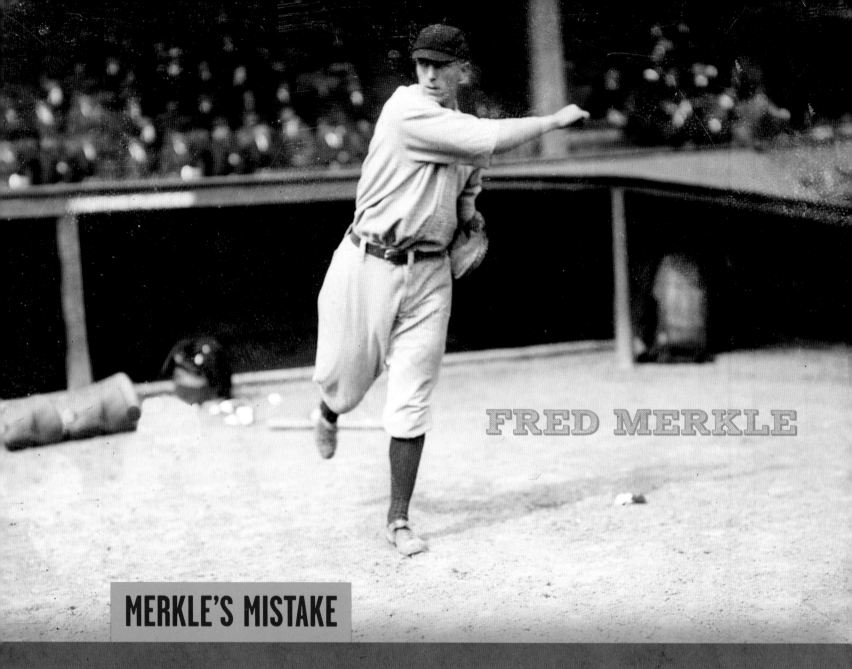

FRED MERKLE

MERKLE'S MISTAKE

In 1908, the Giants and the Chicago Cubs were in a close battle for the NL pennant. On September 23, the two clubs faced off in a tense game in New York that was tied 1–1 in the bottom of the ninth inning. With two runners on base, Giants shortstop Al Bridwell came to the plate and cracked the game-winning hit. Or so many people thought. Jubilant Giants fans stormed the field as soon as they realized Bridwell's swing was a hit. Little-used Giants first baseman Fred Merkle, running from first base, thought the game was over and headed for the dugout, never touching second base. The quick-thinking Cubs found the ball and tagged second, prompting the umpires to call Merkle out. Between screaming fans and a riotous Giants dugout, order could not be restored on the field, and the umps declared the game a 1–1 tie. When the two teams ended the season with identical 98–55 records, they were forced to break the tie with a one-game playoff for the pennant. This time, the Cubs got off to an early lead and won 4–2 to capture their third straight league title.

Mel Ott (below) generated uncanny power from his 170-pound frame, becoming the smallest of baseball's all-time great sluggers.

capturing the NL pennant by five games over the Pittsburgh Pirates. Then they dominated the Senators in the World Series, four games to one, with Hubbell winning twice and Schumacher once. New York was back on top.

Under Terry's guidance, the Giants won two more NL pennants in 1936 and 1937 but fell to the Yankees in the World Series each year. It would be 14 years before the Polo Grounds would host another championship battle.

THE THREE M'S

ew baseball experts would have predicted that the Giants would reach the World Series in 1951. Trailing the NL-leading Brooklyn Dodgers by 13 games in mid-August, New York staged a miraculous late-season comeback to force a three-game playoff series with the Dodgers for the NL pennant. The dramatic series went down to the bottom of the ninth inning of Game 3 with the Dodgers leading 4–2. Then, Giants third baseman Bobby Thomson crushed a game-winning, three-run homer. As Thomson danced around the bases with the pennant-winning run, exuberant Giants radio announcer Russ Hodges shouted into his microphone, "The Giants win the pennant! The Giants win the pennant! I don't believe it! I do not believe it!"

The Giants lost the 1951 World Series to the crosstown Yankees, but fans would witness the unbelievable again three years later, when young superstar center fielder Willie Mays led New York to another world championship in 1954. The Giants' adversaries, the Cleveland Indians, were heavily favored to win that year's World Series, but

THIRD BASEMAN · DARRELL EVANS

Pitchers knew better than to give Darrell Evans good pitches to swing at; he twice led the NL in walks. Yet Evans still became the first player in major-league history to hit 40 or more homers in a season in both leagues. Hitting a home run was the best feeling in the world for Evans. "It's what you live for. Sometimes it is what you die for," he said. "You put one up there, and it makes you feel young again." To prove his point, at age 38, as a member of the Detroit Tigers, Evans pounded 40 dingers to capture the AL home run crown.

STATS

Giants seasons: 1976–83

Height: 6-foot-2

Weight: 205

- **2,223 career hits**
- **2-time All-Star**
- **1,605 career walks**
- **414 career HR**

DARRELL EVANS
THIRD BASEMAN

SAN FRANCISCO
GIANTS

THOMSON'S SHOT

Down by 13 games in the NL standings in mid-August, things weren't looking good for the 1951 Giants. But then the team went on a historic tear, winning 16 consecutive games and 37 of its final 44. The feat led to a best-of-three playoff series for the pennant against the Giants' rival, the Brooklyn Dodgers. After splitting the first two games, the teams headed into Game 3. In the ninth inning of Game 3, the Giants were in their final at bat and down 4–2. With two Giants players on base, Dodgers hurler Ralph Branca threw a strike on the outside corner to Giants third baseman Bobby Thomson. The second pitch was up and inside. The third toss was a breaking ball, down and away—a bad pitch that Thomson swung at anyway. Thomson miraculously connected and yanked the ball down the left-field line. The ball kept sailing until it dropped into the stands just over the fence. The homer, which won the Giants not only the game but the NL pennant as well, is remembered as "The Shot Heard 'Round the World" and marked one of the most dramatic playoff moments in baseball history.

Mays had other ideas. In Game 1, with the score tied 2–2 in the eighth and two Cleveland runners on base, Indians first baseman Vic Wertz belted the ball to the deepest part of center field. But the graceful center fielder outran the ball, made an amazing over-the-shoulder catch, then slung the ball back to the infield, saving at least two runs. Mays's catch took the wind out of the Indians' sails, and the Giants romped to the championship in four straight games.

Starting with that 1954 World Series, Mays quickly established himself as one of the best and most popular players in the major leagues. Giants manager Leo Durocher knew he had a special star on his hands right away. "He could do the five things you have to do to be a superstar: hit, hit with power, run, throw, and field," the skipper marveled. "And he had that other ingredient that turns a superstar into a super superstar. He lit up the room when he came in. He was a joy to be around."

Unfortunately, New York fans got to watch Mays perform for only a few years. By 1958, declining attendance at the Polo Grounds led Giants owner Horace Stoneham to move his team to San Francisco, where he hoped to build a larger fan base. As they settled into Seals Stadium, the Giants welcomed several new players. Rookie Felipe Alou manned the outfield with Mays, and newcomer Orlando Cepeda took over at first base. The next year, Cepeda shifted to the outfield to make room for rookie first baseman Willie "Stretch" McCovey, who quickly displayed both fearsome hitting and graceful fielding.

In 1960, the Giants moved into a new stadium, Candlestick Park, on the western shore of San Francisco Bay, where the swirling winds in the outfield often wreaked havoc on fly balls. Local fans also began cheering for a new pitching star, high-kicking right-hander Juan Marichal. A native of the Dominican Republic, Marichal had three things a great pitcher needs: speed, control, and confidence. After Marichal threw a one-hitter his first time on the mound in Candlestick Park, sportswriters asked if he was surprised at how well he had performed. With Cepeda translating, Marichal replied in Spanish, "No, I expected to win. I always expect to win."

The three M's—Mays, McCovey, and Marichal—became the nucleus of an NL powerhouse. When future Hall of Fame pitcher Gaylord Perry was added in 1962, the Giants surged to the pennant with a 103–62 mark. Although San Francisco battled for seven games in the World Series, the trophy went back east with its old rivals, the Yankees.

Juan Marichal's high-kicking delivery was one of the most distinctive in the game and helped him hide the ball from batters as long as possible.

SHORTSTOP · GEORGE DAVIS

Switch hitter George Davis seemed to always get on base, either with a hit or a walk. Then he'd steal the next base if a pitcher didn't pay close attention. Davis arrived in New York with a bang in 1893. He hit in 33 straight games (then a big-league record), smacked 27 triples, and drove in 119 runs. Davis had Hall of Fame credentials but earned a reputation as a troublemaker in 1903 when he signed with an AL team and then sued for the right to return to the Giants. The controversy may help to explain why he wasn't inducted into the Hall for almost a century.

GEORGE DAVIS
SHORTSTOP

SAN FRANCISCO
GIANTS

STATS

Giants seasons: 1893–1901, 1903

Height: 5-foot-9

Weight: 180

- 2,665 career hits

- 619 career stolen bases

- .295 career BA

- Baseball Hall of Fame inductee (1998)

SHAKING UP THE NL WEST

T he Giants spent the rest of the 1960s near the top of the NL standings. Mays continued to thrill fans with his booming bat and slick fielding, McCovey ranked among the league's home run leaders every year, and Marichal won 20 or more games nearly every season. Other standouts of that period included outfielder Bobby Bonds, a top home run hitter and base stealer, and lefty Mike McCormick, who, in 1967, became the first Giants pitcher to win the Cy Young Award as the league's best hurler.

In 1969, the NL split into two divisions, with the Giants going into the NL Western Division. San Francisco came in second and third its first two seasons in the NL West, then edged out the Los Angeles Dodgers for the division crown in 1971. In the postseason, the Giants quickly fell to the Pittsburgh Pirates, who went on to claim the World Series title.

During the next 15 years, the Giants enjoyed their share of highlights but failed to reach the playoffs again. Shortstop Chris Speier and

LEFT FIELDER · BARRY BONDS

Barry Bonds had baseball in his blood. The son of major-league outfielder Bobby Bonds and godson of the legendary Willie Mays, Barry became a 7-time NL MVP and 14-time All-Star. Bonds was an outstanding fielder, but he truly made his fame with his bat. During his career, he broke more longstanding offensive records than any other player. In 2003, he became the only player in history to claim 500 homers and 500 stolen bases. In 2007, he became the all-time home run king, finishing his career with 762. "The rest of us play in the major leagues," said Giants shortstop Rich Aurilia. "He's at another level."

BARRY BONDS
LEFT FIELDER

SAN FRANCISCO
GIANTS

STATS

Giants seasons: 1993–2007

Height: 6-foot-1

Weight: 225

• 8-time Gold Glove winner

• 73 home runs in 2001 (most all-time)

• 514 career stolen bases

• 1,996 career RBI

DIFFERENT COAST, SAME STORY

Just four years after moving to San Francisco, the Giants found themselves facing off against the New York Yankees—the team that had four times beaten the Giants for the world championship—in the 1962 World Series. The first six games produced alternating wins, but the first four innings of Game 7 produced nothing. The Yanks managed to put a run on the board in the fifth, but the Giants' pitching staff refused to relinquish any more. The bottom of the ninth was do-or-die for San Francisco. Giants outfielder Matty Alou led off the inning with a pinch-hit bunt, but Yankees hurler Ralph Terry then struck out the next two San Francisco batters. Alou was still stranded at first as center fielder Willie Mays stepped to the plate. Mays belted a double to right field, but Yankees outfielder Roger Maris chased down the ball and fired it to third, preventing Alou from scoring. When first baseman Willie McCovey came to bat, the tension was thick in Candlestick Park. On the third pitch, McCovey hit a screaming line drive, but Yankees second baseman Bobby Richardson snagged it for the final out, giving New York its 20th World Series title and depriving the Giants of their first championship in San Francisco.

WILL CLARK

second baseman Tito Fuentes turned over one dynamic double play after another during these years. And in 1976, cocky pitcher John "The Count" Montefusco tossed a no-hitter against the Atlanta Braves.

In 1981, the Giants made headlines when baseball legend Frank Robinson took the helm, becoming the first African American manager in the NL. But even Robinson's immense knowledge and experience couldn't pull San Francisco up in the standings. The team hit rock bottom in 1985, suffering the first 100-loss season in franchise history. Former Giants pitcher Roger Craig then took over as manager and announced, "We're going to get back to the basics. If we can discipline ourselves to do the little things right, the big things will take care of themselves."

Craig got down to basics with a whole new infield that featured slick-fielding Will "The Thrill" Clark at first base and the reliable double-play combination of second baseman Robby Thompson and shortstop Jose Uribe. Craig blended youngsters and veterans with stunning success the next year, propelling the team to its first division title since 1971. Two years later, San Francisco topped the NL West again, defeated the Chicago Cubs in the NL Championship Series (NLCS), and took on the Oakland A's in the first-ever Bay Area World Series. The Giants lost the first

Six-time All-Star Will Clark won both the Gold Glove and Silver Slugger awards in 1991 as the NL's best defensive and offensive first baseman.

GIANTS

[33]

two games but were confident heading into Game 3. However, just half an hour before the game was scheduled to start, a major earthquake rocked the Bay Area, damaging Candlestick Park and postponing the game for 10 days. The Giants never recovered, losing the series in four games.

San Francisco went into a downward spiral as the 1990s began, attendance fell dramatically, and rumors spread that the franchise might move to Florida. Then a new ownership group took over and promised to turn the club around. Craig was replaced as manager in 1993 by Dusty Baker, and multitalented outfielder Barry Bonds—a two-time NL MVP—was signed to a big free-agent contract. Bonds had deep ties to the Giants: his father Bobby had been a Giants star in the 1960s, and Willie Mays was his godfather. In his first year in San Francisco, Bonds showcased his awesome offensive skills by swiping 29 bases, jacking 46 homers, and driving in 123 runs. With the help of pitchers John Burkett and Bill Swift, who each logged more than 20 wins, the Giants won 103 games and finished a close second in the NL West.

Baker kept the team near the top of the standings for much of the '90s, with Bonds and new stars such as second baseman Jeff Kent and first

CENTER FIELDER · WILLIE MAYS

Willie Mays was the original "five-tool" player—he fielded brilliantly, made laser throws, stole bases, hit for average, and hit for power. A 2-time NL MVP, Mays earned 12 Gold Gloves as the league's best defensive center fielder and is the only player ever to record 600 homers, 300 stolen bases, and 3,000 hits. "He would routinely do things you never saw anyone else do," said Giants president Peter McGowan. "He'd score from first base on a single. He'd take two bases on a pop-up. He'd throw somebody out at the plate on one bounce. And the bigger the game, the better he played."

WILLIE MAYS
CENTER FIELDER

SAN FRANCISCO GIANTS

STATS

Giants seasons: 1951–72

Height: 5-foot-11

Weight: 180

- **3,283 career hits**

- **20-time All-Star**

- **2,062 career runs scored**

- **Baseball Hall of Fame inductee (1979)**

baseman J. T. Snow leading the offense. The Giants won division titles in both 1997 and 2000, the same year they moved into their new home, Pacific Bell Park (known as AT&T Park as of 2010). Unfortunately, they failed to reach the World Series each time. San Francisco fans wondered if their hopes for a championship would finally be realized in the new millennium.

TURNING UP THE POWER

Barry Bonds ushered in the new millennium with an unprecedented show of power. In 2001, he slammed 73 round-trippers to break the single-season home run record of 70, established a few years earlier by St. Louis Cardinals slugger Mark McGwire. "This was one of the greatest years—no, it was *the* greatest year—I have seen from a single person," said Baker. Bonds's 46 homers and league-leading .370 average the next year helped propel the team to an NL Wild Card berth and eventually to the World Series. There, the Giants battled the Anaheim Angels to a deciding Game 7 before finally succumbing.

Bonds helped lead the Giants to another NL West title in 2003 and

BARRY BONDS

then made headlines in 2004 as well, earning his fourth-straight NL
MVP award and becoming only the third player in history to break the
700-homer mark. Over the next few seasons, he would continue to pound
the baseball, surpassing first Babe Ruth and then Hank Aaron to become
baseball's all-time home run king.

But Bonds's accomplishments were tempered by controversy.
Rumors had long swirled that the San Francisco slugger had used
steroids or other performance-enhancing drugs to illegally build up

JACK CLARK

THE NINE-DAY GAME

When the Giants played the Chicago Cubs on July 20, 1978, it was San Francisco's last scheduled trip to Wrigley Field for the season. The Cubs got on the board first by scoring two runs in the first inning. The two teams battled back and forth, and by the end of the seventh inning, the game was tied 8–8. In the first half of the eighth inning, the Giants managed a single, a sacrifice bunt, and a ground out before right fielder Jack Clark singled to left, giving San Francisco a 9–8 lead. But the game, which started at 3:16 P.M., was running a little long. When the Giants scored their ninth run in the eighth inning, it was 6:34 P.M. And shadows were creeping across the field. Since Wrigley Field did not have outside lighting, the game was suspended until the next time the two teams met. So, on July 28, the Giants and Cubs set up shop again, this time in San Francisco's Candlestick Park. They picked up right where they had left off, down to the same lineups. Neither team scored during the remaining 10 outs, and the Giants ended up with baseball's most drawn-out win ever.

RIGHT FIELDER · MEL OTT

"Master Melvin" was a fan favorite during his 22 years with the Giants. When Ott came to the organization in 1926 as a scrawny 17-year-old, his unusual style of lifting his right foot before smashing his bat into the pitch amazed onlookers with its effectiveness—it always seemed as if he would miss the ball entirely. Ott was the first NL player to rack up 500 home runs and recorded 8 years with 30 or more dingers. Twice in his career he was walked six times in a doubleheader. From 1942 to 1948, Ott also managed the team (continuing for a year after he stopped playing).

MEL OTT
RIGHT FIELDER

SAN FRANCISCO
GIANTS

STATS

Giants seasons: 1926–47 (as player), 1942–48 (as manager)

Height: 5-foot-9

Weight: 170

- **12-time All-Star**

- **511 career HR**

- **.304 career BA**

- **Baseball Hall of Fame inductee (1951)**

MANAGER · JOHN McGRAW

The demanding man known as "Little Napoleon" became the winningest manager in Giants history and the second-winningest manager in baseball history. During McGraw's lengthy tenure, the Giants finished in first or second place 20 times. He developed several strategic plays that managers still use, such as the hit-and-run and the squeeze play (in which the batter bunts so that the runner on third base can score). McGraw always made sure his players knew who was in charge. "With my team I am an absolute czar," he once admitted. "My men know it. I order plays and they obey."

JOHN McGRAW
MANAGER

SAN FRANCISCO
GIANTS

STATS

Giants seasons as manager:
   1902–32

Managerial record: 2,763–1,948

World Series championships:
   1905, 1921, 1922

Baseball Hall of Fame inductee
   (1937)

his body and his strength. As a result, many fans and baseball experts refused to recognize his achievements. Bonds denied using steroids in testimony before a grand jury in 2003 and was later indicted for perjury, or lying under oath. The case was postponed for many years but remained a cloud over Bonds and professional baseball. Bonds left the Giants after his contract expired in 2007 but did not officially retire until 2009.

As Bonds was ending his Giants career, the club's pitching experienced a major revival. First, sidewinder Barry Zito was signed to a big free-agent contract; then, new young arms such as Matt Cain, Tim Lincecum, and Jonathan Sanchez were brought up from the minor leauges. By 2008, the Giants featured perhaps the best pitching staff in the NL, and Lincecum established himself as the top starter in the league. Using a herky-jerky motion and deceptive speed, Lincecum would freeze batters in place and then mow them down. "He's got some of the nastiest stuff I've ever seen," said Houston

MATT CAIN

Astros outfielder Hunter Pence. Lincecum won 18 games in 2008 and 15 in 2009, led the league in strikeouts both years, and earned 2 consecutive NL Cy Young Awards.

Giants management also focused on improving the team's offense, trading for veteran outfielder Aaron Rowland and infielder Juan Uribe. But the real find was a budding young superstar—third baseman Pablo Sandoval. Built more like a football linebacker than a baseball player, Sandoval brought talent and enthusiasm with him when he arrived in San Francisco in 2008.

Sandoval and his teammates improved to 88–74 in 2009. Then, in 2010, they won the NL West on the final day of the season. That's when they really got hot. Behind the sensational pitching of Lincecum, Cain, and bearded closer Brian Wilson, and with the slugging of first baseman Aubrey Huff and eye-opening play of rookie catcher Buster Posey, San Francisco flattened the Atlanta Braves and Philadelphia Phillies in the playoffs to win the NL pennant. There was no stopping the Giants in the World Series, as they knocked off the Texas Rangers in 5 games to win their first world championship in 56 years. "San Francisco is going nuts," said a jubilant Wilson, who notched a strikeout for the Series' final out. "We're going nuts, and it feels really good."

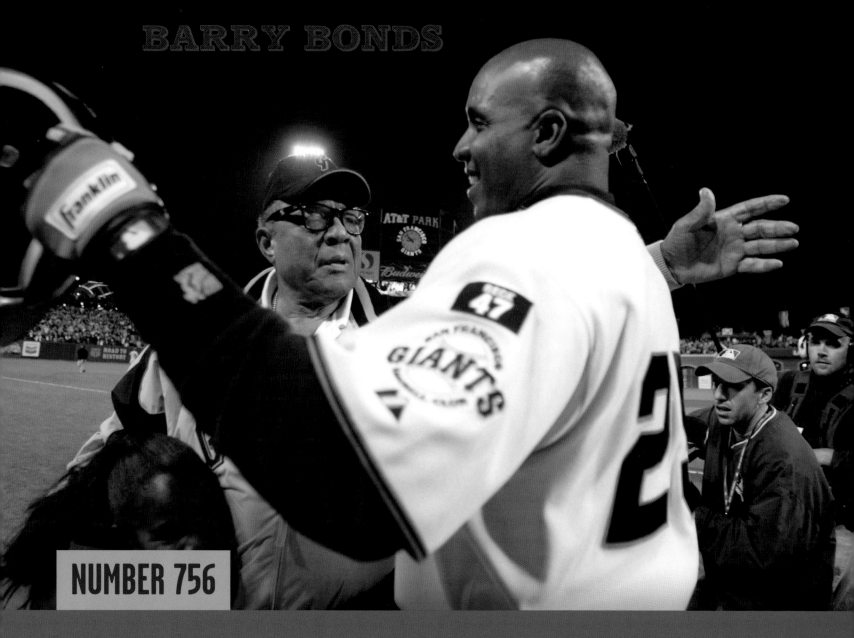

BARRY BONDS

NUMBER 756

As a boy, watching his father Bobby Bonds and godfather Willie Mays, Barry Bonds dreamed about becoming baseball's all-time home run king. Then, starting in the year 2001, he began a serious drive to topple Hank Aaron's record of 755 homers. Bonds hit his 500th shot in April 2001, his 600th in August 2002, and his 700th in September 2004 (averaging almost 50 homers a year). Then age and injury began to rob the outfielder of some of his power. On August 7, 2007, Bonds finally cracked number 756 to the deepest part of Pacific Bell Park. He raised his hands in triumph and circled the bases with feelings of both excitement and relief. "I knew I hit it," Bonds said. "I knew I got it. I was like, *phew*, finally." San Francisco fans gave their hero a long standing ovation, and a taped message from Aaron was played on the stadium video board. "I have been privileged to hold this record for 33 years," Aaron said. "I move over now and offer my best wishes to Barry and his family on this historic achievement. My hope today … is that the achievement of this record will inspire others to chase their own dreams."

GIANTS

Nicknamed "The Freak," long-haired ace Tim Lincecum stood a slight 5-foot-11 but fired with the velocity of a much larger pitcher.

TIM LINCECUM

PABLO SANDOVAL

Pablo Sandoval (opposite), Buster Posey, Brian Wilson, Aubrey Huff (below, left to right), and the rest of the Giants shocked the sports world in 2010.

For more than 125 years, the Giants have been thrilling fans on both the East Coast and the West Coast with exciting baseball. Their history echoes from the old Polo Grounds to the modern AT&T Park and includes 6 World Series trophies and 55 Hall of Fame inductees. Those numbers are sure to rise in the decades to come, and Giants fans are already looking forward to the day their heroes will bring that next championship home to the golden city of San Francisco.

GIANTS

INDEX